Other books By JoAnne Smith Hooks

I Don't Take It Lightly
&
The Root of Bitterness – Workbook

Published by: Cree Publishing Company
In: 2006 & 2008

A Bitter Disease Called Unforgiveness

JoAnne Smith Hooks

WestBow
PRESS
A DIVISION OF THOMAS NELSON

WestBow Press books may be ordered through booksellers or by contacting:

WestBow Press
A Division of Thomas Nelson
1663 Liberty Drive
Bloomington, IN 47403
www.westbowpress.com
1-(866) 928-1240

Because of the dynamic nature of the Internet, any web addresses or
links contained in this book may have changed since publication and
may no longer be valid. The views expressed in this work are solely those
of the author and do not necessarily reflect the views of the publisher,
and the publisher hereby disclaims any responsibility for them.

Any people depicted in stock imagery provided by Thinkstock are
models, and such images are being used for illustrative purposes only.

Certain stock imagery © Thinkstock.

ISBN: 978-1-4497-3547-0 (sc)
ISBN: 978-1-4497-3546-3 (e)

Library of Congress Control Number: 2011963340

Printed in the United States of America

WestBow Press rev. date: 1/03/2012

Dedicated

To God The Father, His Son Jesus and The Holy Ghost!

Since my book back in 2006 based on, "I Don't Take It Lightly" and the Workbook on the, "Root of Bitterness in 2008 God has added two little lively boys to our family. They have won my heart. They are my Great-Grandsons, Kahmari Jolee'n & Kahlil Tay'Shawn. I would like to dedicate this book to them, my son Chester and my grand children, Chaquita, Rodney, Carrie, Anthony and Lamont.

To my husband, Lee Andrew Hooks, has supported me in all my endeavors over a period of thirty years.
Thank you for your support!

Without these two people in my life showing inspiration, it would have been difficult to pursue my dreams!

My 94-year-old mom, Willie Mae Smith
In memory of my dad, Wesley Smith

To my only biological child that God has blessed me with and I do not take it lightly! She has inspired me to keep writing. I love you!

Shauntae!

Acknowledgements

To my Biological Brothers and Sisters who never stopped believing in me.

I love you family and I thank you for supporting me . . .
Our Father told us before God took him home to always know
"where your siblings are". God has blessed fourteen of us out of twenty,
as well as our 94-year-old Mom to still be on this earth
and we "Don't Take It Lightly".

To my nieces and nephews, great, cousins and there are truly many.
I love you all so much!

To my First Publisher of, "I Don't Take It Lightly
& The Root of Bitterness"
Conita Jones
Thank you for the patience that you have with me, as well as
encouraging me to continue to write.

Louise Mothershed
Thank you for being a friend that sticks by my side and
speaks only positive words into my life.

Deborah Holmes
Thank you for being a very special person in my life.
You are a woman that truly walks by faith and not by sight.

Edna Johnson
Thank you for true friendship.
Each day I learn that friends are a gift from God.

Sheila Cooper
You are a friend that will take the coat off your back
when seeing a need. I love you Ms. Sheila.

Rebecca Shields
You are a woman of wisdom and knowledge.
Thank you Becky for your friendship.

To my spiritual daughter Lynette Davis
Thank you for bringing sunshine into my life.

To my:
spiritual daughters Cynthia Hawkins,
Denise Hardaway & Denise McKnight
Thank you for your love and kindness and sticking with
me from the first day that we met.

Dorothy Gift
To my Bestest Friend. Thank you for supporting me in everything
that God has given me to do. You are a great person!

Valena Burkes
Thank you for staying by my side to encourage me on a daily basis.
You are the best my friend!

To:
Andrea Rich, Joann Sullivan, Shirley Mitchell, Judy Patterson, Ethel
Swenson, Stephanie Springs, CeCe Gray, Janie Bell, Rosaline Jones,
Shirley Richardson, Teri Fort, Kim Taylor and Joyce Latimer
Thank you all for all your hard work, loyalty and friendship. "We will
always be Women of Vision". I love you . . .

From the Author

Dear Readers,

I am inspired once again, by the Holy Ghost to write this particular book based on Bitterness. There was a picture presented to me one day by a young lady with several scriptures on it. This picture's author or writer were considered unknown. I know it was God—sent for me. She had no idea that this was a breaking point that I needed to close some chapters in my life.

I started thinking about all the things that had made me bitter toward others, especially those that had wronged me down through the years. I couldn't understand why it was so difficult for me to shake certain images out of my mind.

I remember many years ago when I started crying out to God for true deliverance. As I prayed day after day, month after month and year after year seeking God for answers to my problems, He gave me the solution.

One day as I was preparing for a speaking engagement I heard the Holy Spirit telling me, to share a particular thing with His people. I actually said, "No Lord, please don't make me do that". He assured me that if I shared it I would be delivered. The title of the message was, "Lord Deliver Me". I thought the message was only for me but it was also for those that were in the congregation, as well. I want you to know things are going to come up in your life and people are going to do you wrong but the key is, not to allow anything to fester because when it does it can cause you to become bitter. Shake it off before it begins to sprout. Please trust me when I say this. It is not worth you losing sleep over it.

I would like to encourage you if there is bitterness in your heart toward anyone about anything it is time to forgive and let it go. If you don't, it will slowly take a toll on you. It will make you feel like parasites are eating away every organ in your body at a slow pace. I am a living witness. Let it go . . .

This book is based mostly upon un-forgiveness versus forgiveness. In order to forgive, you must strip yourself of all the bitter roots. The Bible says, "Do unto others as you will have them to do unto you."

I pray that the Anointing of God will fall upon you as you read this book through the power of the Holy Ghost. Remember, you have to let it go. You can be free if you just believe . . .

God bless you and be encouraged . . .

Love you,
JoAnne Smith Hooks

Contents

Introduction

Looking back on my life I was labeled as a dreamer. While others were outside playing, I would be inside daydreaming. What's so ironic about my daydreaming is that I would visualize myself in large settings, speaking and preaching to others. Feeling as though nothing of this magnitude could ever happen to a little country girl coming out of the fields of Marianna, Arkansas, when those thoughts occurred, I would say to myself, "JoAnne, get a grip; it's only a dream." Not only that, I couldn't speak that well because of a speech impediment.

I realize now that these were visions that came strictly from God. Some have come to pass and some are still in the making. This is to encourage young people to "hold on to your dreams." Only God will give you pure and holy thoughts. An evil thought comes from the enemy.

Through prayer over the years, God has granted me every thing that I've asked for. We were taught by our mom to get on our knees and pray and many of us have not ceased to pray that way. My mom still prays on her knees at the age of 94. For some reason, this is where our strength lies and the teaching has always been honored. So many of our children today do not know how to pray because they have not been taught, not even the Lord's Prayer.

I've heard people say, "God doesn't answer a sinner's prayer." I have questioned God about this by saying, "God how can this be, if a sinner is asking you to save them? So God, how then can you not answer a sinner's prayer?" I thank God for Salvation. Be careful my friend of the company that you keep. They may lead you astray.

God has given me a compassionate heart for His people. One of the things that truly disturb me is when they are mistreated, specifically children and the elderly, who are meek, humble and helpless. It's devastating to hear of someone being abused, neglected, rejected, belittled, discredited and mocked. I know, without a doubt, that God is not pleased with those actions, and judgment day is coming for those that wrong others.

I believe this is why God has allowed me to write this book for such a time as this. It's grievous to see so much bitterness, animosity, jealousy, hatred and cruelty in some people. It truly makes my heart ache. The thing that gets me the most is that they say they love the Lord. If we truly loved God with all our heart, soul, mind and strength we wouldn't mistreat others.

We seem to forget that there is a heaven and there is a hell. Time is truly coming to an end for each and every one of us, yet God is giving us time now to repent. The Bible says, "Repent for the kingdom of heaven is at hand." It is not too late to turn your life over to Christ. Don't put off for tomorrow what you can do today.

I pray that this book will be a blessing to you and your family . . .

CHAPTER 1
Hidden Roots

As we explore the hidden roots in our lives I would like to bring to your attention that it is a root that cannot be seen. It is hidden from view, but will eventually spring up and defile you. When you are sick, you often ask why has this sickness come upon me? Some time it springs up from bitterness. Some of the fruits of bitterness can be seen through cancer, arthritis and rheumatism.

Bitterness also results in the heart turning away from God, in hardness of the heart, bitterness toward God for misfortunes in life, and not appropriating God's grace.

Other manifestation of bitterness include envy and strife; sharp and bitter words; and complaining.

Growing up in a large family of 20 siblings there was always envy and strife in the camp. That's just what siblings do. We were competitive and there was always one that caused discord in the camp, especially if they weren't happy. As we get older those things are supposed to cease. Perhaps some of us will never grow up. Whatever we did during our childhood days we bring it into our adult lives.

We often see this in our society today as more than ever our sons and daughters are still living with their parents and causing discord on every hand. It is a sad situation that our children have no desire to work, yet they will stay home all day long watching television, playing video games, bringing their friends over and expecting us to cater to their "wants." Not their needs, but their "wants." We are losing this generation to the enemy and we can't see that our children are hurting because we are so wrapped up in our lives with envy, strife and bitterness that it's difficult for us to see their hurts. We are training our children to be just like us, and God is not pleased with some of our actions.

We go to church every Sunday, praising God throughout the service and leaving the same way we came in. Some of us have no desire to get delivered and we don't want to see others delivered, either.

It is truly hard to understand the mentality of God's people when it comes to the sharp and bitter words. It is as though they are getting pleasure from finding ways to hurt people. What happened to humility and love? Have we forgotten that we are to love our brother and sister as Christ loves us? Or better yet, have we forgotten where God has brought us?

How dare we forget that some of us were caught up in drugs, alcohol, abuse, prostitution, pornography, strip joints, prisons, adultery, lust, living in homeless shelters, sleeping in cars and lying in the streets or sleeping on cardboard boxes. Some of us were liars, thieves, backstabbers, backbiters; robbers, con artists, gossipers, etc . . . and we take it upon ourselves to turn our heads from others when we see and hear that they are hurting or are in the same situation. God forbid . . .

In addition, we have concluded that it's going to be our way or no way. God is not pleased with our actions. In some instances, we get angry with our brother or sister and feel it is our responsibility not to speak to them. We go on as though nothing is wrong or worse, we say, "Oh well, they will get over it". This is where un-forgiveness comes in, which leads straight to bitterness.

A person has to forgive in order to break the power of bitterness. The Bible says, "Do not let the sun go down on your wrath." We are also told to forgive. Even part of the Lord's Prayer says, "Forgive us our trespasses (sin) as we forgive those who trespass against us." Why is this so difficult for us to do?

We are supposed to go to our brother or sister and ask them, "If I have offended you in any way will you please find in it in your heart to forgive me?" This is Biblical. It shouldn't matter if the person wronged you. It is you taking pride off your shoulders and allowing God to free you. If you wait on some people to ask you to forgive them, trust me, you will be waiting for a while and you may miss your seat in heaven.

Asking for forgiveness and truly meaning it, is the only way we are going to make it to heaven. When God touched our lives and showed us His beauty, no doubt we all probably used the same line, by saying, "Father, please forgive me, for I am a sinner and have sinned against you. I'm sorry and I want to be saved." Even if we have been in church all our lives, one day we had to get saved. The Bible says, "We are sinners, saved by grace!"

Another thing that God is not pleased with is our complaining . . . He does not want us to complain because He is in control of everything.

Growing up as a young girl, complaining was a big thing with me. Nothing was ever right, and if someone had a task to do, I felt they should have done it better. It wasn't so much that I spoke, but it would definitely be in my mind.

Being a bitter child, hating everything and feeling hatred in my heart against everyone, brought bitterness into my life and at the age of 13, I suffered molestation. This wasn't something that could be erased from my memory overnight, since I was young and dealing with it alone. I was afraid to speak out, thinking, I would be labeled as a nasty and wicked child. So I dealt with it for 40 years, again, all alone. In the year of 2006, my story was exposed to the public in my first book, ("I Don't Take It

Lightly"), which brought healing into my life. Since then there have been so many men, women and children that have begun to speak out to bring healing into their lives.

Hearing some of their stories will break your heart. Some of these women and men are in their late fifties, sixties, seventies and eighties. They are pouring out their hearts telling how their grandfathers, fathers, uncles, brothers, cousins, relatives, friends or neighbors molested them. They were just babies growing up in their homes or neighborhoods. This is why we are finding so many people who are bitter. They have chosen to die with this secret locked up inside of them as opposed to getting delivered. It's because they feel guilty, ashamed or embarrassed. Often their attacker has led them to believe that they are to blame for what took place. I want them to know today, "the devil is a liar." To those that are feeling that way, please rest assured that this was not your fault. You were just a baby and you did what you were told to do. You did it out of fear. Please stop blaming yourself, get some counseling, or find someone that you can confide in.

Please do not continue to harbor this bitterness in your heart. Pull this thing up by the roots and let deliverance take place in your life this day. It is so important to talk with someone. If you do not, this will consume your mind and some of us are not as strong as others. Here's a portion of my story . . . .

My attacker was much older than I, and he was supposed to have been my friend. He took me down the back roads of Arkansas and raped me repeatedly. What puzzled me as I pondered this in my heart for so many years was how he pretended to be my friend and did something so devastating to me. Did he not realize that something of that magnitude would work on my sanity? It is so difficult for me to grasp in my mind that someone could be so devious as to think they had the right to force me to do something against my will. When it comes to preying on sweet innocent children, the elderly or someone that's incapacitated, how, dare they allow Satan to enter into their mind to do such a horrible thing?

My heart ached for 40 years because I did not expose this to anyone. I am not telling you it was an easy task, because it wasn't. I became an alcoholic and lashed out at others, due to bitterness and blaming myself for what took place.

For years, I would drink, to drown the pain that I carried in my heart. It was a pain that was too difficult to share. I discovered if I complained about everything, then no one would question me about anything. I was digging a hole deeper and deeper, yet, I wasn't aware that I would fall into it one day. In my book, "I Don't Take It Lightly" I described why, where, when, and how the incident took place in detail.

The end result of my story is, that through the complaining, bitterness and alcohol, I brought sickness into my body. That was the hole that I dug for myself. Through anger and sin in my life, I was surrounded by darkness. I was actually blinded by Satan for so many years, until I thought that Jesus had forgotten about me. I was crying out to Him on a daily basis, but for some reason I didn't want to let go of all those wrong things that I was doing.

You see, I wanted to have my cake and eat it too! Oh, I could justify my sins. My stories were beyond recognition. My own justification was so clear to me that I started believing it myself, and it became a reality to me. The consequences of my wrongdoing paid off with a warrant trip to a hospice unit, where 3 elderly women and I were placed to die, with a deadly disease called "cancer".

The dictionary says that cancer is an evil condition that spreads destructively. We should truly encourage people to have a colonoscopy done. My doctor assured me that this is an excellent procedure! Frankly, the cleansing part is awesome prior to having the actual procedure done! At the age of 59, I had this procedure done April 2010, as my husband was persisted in getting this checked out. He knew something was wrong. Knowing that it was the Spirit of the Lord speaking to his heart, I believe he saw death in me, because he wouldn't give up. He even made my appointment. It was 35 years ago and I felt that the Spirit of the Lord had spoken to me and told me that no more surgical knives would be laid upon me due to the refusal of a 3rd surgery in 1982. This is why I protested.

After going through the procedure, the doctor detected a Polyp on my intestine that was bringing the cancer back. Yet, that's not the end of the story. They also detected that I had diverticulum. So, you see, I had double trouble. Prior to the procedure, I knew in my heart that I would not be able to survive another 6 months. It had gotten to the place that a huge lump would come under my left arm and I often had to take my right hand to lift up my left arm because of the poor blood circulation. It had actually become dead weight and totally numb at times, and sometimes, painful. I could not sleep for months. Death was on my trail, once again. I could smell the blood in my system yet I refused to tell my husband or my doctor.

I knew it was only a matter of time before I would be vomiting up buckets of blood, again, which I stated in, "I Don't Take It Lightly." I felt as though my suffering days would be over and it was time for me to go home with the Lord. I could actually visualize, as well as feel the cancer, coming back.

My doctor told me after receiving the report, "that it was a very, very nasty Polyp." She said, "it was one of the worst and I was only an inch away from cancer." But God said, "Not so, for He had a plan and purpose for my life." I am so grateful to be here. I am a living witness that God performs miracles!

We know that this disease (cancer) is definitely from the enemy. Remember, the dictionary states, "that it is evil." We must curse this root along with all the other diseases and command them to leave the bodies of God's people. If we come together in prayer and fasting God will bring some changes, not only in our lives, but also in this universe. The Bible says, "One can chase a thousand and two can put ten thousands to flight". Can you imagine if a few or a million of us came together with one accord in fasting and prayer, having no doubts, complaints or negative feelings, just trusting and believing God to put the devil under subjection, what would happen?

Can you believe that God would turn this world upside down? Families would be restored, children would be obedient, prayer would come back into the schools, wars would cease, and drugs and alcohol would not destroy people lives. Can you believe the atmosphere would change because then we would have touched the heart of God and heaven gates would open up? He is calling for a humble people with a humble heart that cares for His people. This is the remnant group that God is looking for, a praying people that will stand only for righteousness, not looking for riches, but for righteousness.

I am a living witness that fasting and prayer does work. I have been living my life for Christ for almost 30 years. The first fifteen years I dedicated every day of my life to Him in fasting in prayer. The last 3 days of every month was an absolute fast with only water. It did not matter what days those 3 days fell on. Even if it was a holiday it did not matter to me. They were given to God for saving, healing and delivering me. He truly did not have to do it, but He had mercy on an old, wretched person like me, and I was grateful then, and I am still grateful today. I will never be able to repay God for all the things He has done for me. I do know this much and that is, I owe Him my life . . .

I am not saying that I am perfect, because I am not. Only Jesus is perfect. The Bible says, "We all sin and fall short of the glory of God." That means none of us have made it. I want you to know within 5 years of dedicating my life to God and standing on the promise that I made to Him, it was phenomenal and He did something miraculous in my life!

You will find out in the next chapter why fasting and praying plays an important role in my life. I must say this. It is 30 years later, and I have not stopped. I have asked God to make fasting as much a part of my life as eating. I heard my older sister, Ethel, use that phrase, and I acted upon it. I said, "If it's working for her surely it will work for me." I can truly say it has brought me closer to God than ever before and has given me a personal relationship with Him. It truly brings humility into one's life.

CHAPTER 2
A Touch of Humility

HUMILITY—IS THE QUALITY OF BEING humble: modest, not proud, doing something out of the goodness of your heart, not for yourself.

In chapter one I told you about being in the hospice unit with three elderly ladies. Let me take you back thirty years ago. This story is told in detail in my book, "I Don't Take It Lightly." Please note:

As I was lying in the hospice unit, flat on my back, waiting to die at the age of 29, I discovered what humility meant. As my life flashed before my face, I came to the reality that this was it, that this wasn't a joke anymore. It wasn't like a bad cold that would pass on after a few days or a headache that would leave in a day or two. I said to myself, "I am truly dying and no one can help me." This one I couldn't blame on anyone. Usually, my parents, my sisters or brothers would come to my rescue and bail me out of all my troubles, but no one could help me this time. It was between God and me. I realized at that precise moment that, I was staring death right in the face. As fear over shadowed me, I came to the conclusion that if God didn't do it, it just wasn't going to happen.

I would like to share with you what happened to me as I was lying in the recovery room just coming out of a 2nd surgery.

I could see 6 doctors discussing my case. I couldn't hear them, but I knew they were talking about me, not knowing they had served a death warrant on my head. As I tell you this portion of my life, you will see why I chose to go into the medical field.

The doctors had their backs turned away from me and since I was heavily sedated, there was a nurse in the room with me. Please listen as I tell you this because it is totally true, and I will never forget it as long as I live. I can remember it as though it happened yesterday, because it was a devastating time for me.

There was a tube that had been inserted through my nose, into my throat, and down into my stomach. This was inserted when I first came through the doors of the hospital and was not removed even during the surgery. This tube helped with the vomiting and bleeding that I had no control over, and I am sure the doctors didn't want to take the chance of removing it before the surgery in case there was a recurrence. That's my assumption. The nurse that was in the room was extremely cruel to me and she knew that I was unable to speak. She also knew that I would not remember her because of the heavy sedation from the medicine. What she did was totally unreal to me. It was an act of evil coming directly from Satan.

She took the tube and shoved it down my throat several times for no apparent reason. She actually turned her back toward me off and on to make sure the doctors weren't aware of what she was doing. I tried to speak as well as raised my hand to try to get the doctors attention. But I was unable to even lift a finger, as I was extremely weak as well. This showed me that she had perfect timing and had done this before to others.

As I began to cry, begging her with my eyes, to please stop, because she was hurting me badly, she started laughing silently. The more the tears flowed from my eyes, the harder she pushed that tube down my nose and throat.

She was pushing and twisting it with every ounce of strength in her body as she laughed. It felt as though every suture/stitch in my stomach was been ripped apart for no apparent reason. The pain was extremely unbearable, until it caused me lose consciousness. No one had to tell me I passed out, it was obviously so.

During that experience the only thing that I could do was pray and asked God to help me and to please come to my rescue. By the grace of God, when I woke up, I had been placed in a room. A few days later I was rolled to hospice . . . .

I reported her but it didn't do any good because no one believed me. There was no report of a nurse being in the room with me while the doctors were in the room. Who would believe someone that was already at death's door anyway? That's my take on it.

I thought about all the poor people who had come and would come, through that hospital and what she had done and would do to them. I would hope that God would have heard my prayers for the sake of others because there are truly some cruel people in this world.

Yet, there wasn't much that I could say even with that punishment, because I hadn't treated people too kindly before I got sick. I believe the old saying is still true today, "What goes around comes around." I'm a firm believer that we will reap what we sow and we will get double for our trouble whether we are saints or sinners if we have wronged or hurt someone.

After that humility took place in my life, I chose to go into the medical field because I realized that I cared about what happened to people, after all the things I had experienced. I asked God to let no one experience what I have gone through. I would never wish that upon anyone. Some things we truly bring upon ourselves. And I know that my sickness came from a sinful lifestyle.

I also asked God to let no one ever experience the cancer battle that I have gone through, due to the excruciating pain that penetrated my body, and affected my mind on a daily basis. Remember, I shared with you that I was vomiting up buckets of blood off and on for a period of nine months, before they discovered what was actually wrong with me. I definitely would like to share with you that I had no Radiation or Chemotherapy.

This is why my messages are based upon healing and deliverance because God is the Ultimate Healer and Deliverer. I must tell you that I honestly know what it is like to have the ability to endure pain through suffering. I am a firm believer that, if God will take you through it, He will surely bring you out of it.

I am sure you have come to the conclusion that God healed me of the cancer. Within 5 years of my prayer and fasting life, God chose to heal me. He did not have to, but He chose to, and I am truly grateful.

Frankly, I didn't even realize when it happened. I was just so glad to be on the field working for the Lord that I failed to realize that I was sick. One day I woke up and the problem was gone. I went back to the doctor 5 years later and he told me that I was in the best of health, and to keep doing what I was doing.

After coming out of hospice, and being sent home to die, I made a vow to get it right with everyone that I thought I had offended. It took me days and months to contact different ones, but I was determined to mend my relationships, regardless of whether they accepted my forgiveness or not.

I realized one thing, if I didn't see anything else, that all the bitterness I was harboring had disappeared. The moral to the story is, as long as you get it right, this will give you a chance to see Jesus' face.

Of course, that was 31 years ago and times have changed. We have doctors and nurses that truly have compassion for their patients. I can attest to having one of the best primary physicians in the world. She is the most caring and compassionate doctor that I have ever met. She spends times with her patients and listens to our problems. Trust me, she is not the ordinary doctor. She has a heart for God's people. All the doctors and staff are extremely kind and care deeply for every patient that comes into the facility.

I would like for you to know that I have forgiven the nurse that did me wrong. If I knew who she was and saw her in person I would truly let her know this. This is the same way I feel about my attacker that raped me in 1964. I have forgiven him as well. What's so ironic, God erased his face from my mind. If I passed him on the streets and he spoke to me I wouldn't recognize him. Those memories are dead roots, old ones at that, and I have no intentions of reviving dead roots. God has given me a forgiving spirit and I forgive those that have wronged me. I hold no grudge against anyone and I refuse to retaliate because this is not the way of the Lord. God said that, "He would fight my battles." I stand on that promise and I take God at His Word.

Look how simple this is: Forgiveness refers to blotting out our sin and guilt. After this happens, the person who did wrong can again be a friend with the one he or she did the wrong to. All of us have sinned against God. There is not one of us who can say that we have not sinned. If we attempt to say that, "then we are a liar and the truth is not in us."

If we are to be friends with God and enjoy His love and kindness, then God will forgive us. When we do wrong things to each other, forgiveness cannot really come until the person who did wrong is willing to pay his debt or make up in any way he can for what he did. However, there is no way we can make up to God for our sins.

Jesus came to pay our debt. He gave His life in our place so we could be friends with God. Our sins and guilt have been blotted (wiped) out if we let Jesus take our place. Jesus said, "that God does not forgive our sins unless we are willing to forgive one another."

It's just that simple. We must realize that an unforgiving spirit will not get us to heaven. Harboring un-forgiveness will only lead to bitterness and bitterness causes diseases . . .

CHAPTER 3

Introduction
Can you name this Disease?

I N THIS PARTICULAR CHAPTER I would like to share with you a message that God gave me that touched not only my heart but the hearts of many people, as well . . . Please try and figure out what type of disease this is by the end of this introduction. The actual message will follow . . . Here we go . . .

It starts off by saying: There is a serious issue going on that's causing great stress not only in the world but also among our leaders. It is an issue that is so devastating that it is actually consuming our minds. It is truly a disease.

As we look at the definition of what diseases are: The Bible dictionary says, "they were sickness and common in the Bible times. They were usually described rather than named. It is said, "that diseases affect how people think, feel, and their health.

This particular disease is something that can hold us back from escaping the corruption of sin and living for God. It comes in many forms, such as: bitterness, hatred, malice, holding grudges and resentment. This disease can block God from our lives and provide a foothold for the devil to influence us. It can plant a "root of bitterness" in us that leads to damaging results. It can ruin the fruit of the Holy Ghost, stunt your spiritual growth and contribute to physical illness. Just like acid can destroy the vessel that holds it, so can this disease destroy us when we hold on to it.

This disease can harm: Our physical health, disrupt our mental being, and most of all hinder our Spiritual walk with God. Now I ask you the question: What disease am I talking about?

_____.

If you haven't figured it out perhaps, you will know what it is at the end of the message . . .

CHAPTER 4

The Message
The Sycamine Tree

THIS MESSAGE IS PLACED IN the form of a story because I am called the "Storyteller," the Evangelist that tells the story. Jesus was classified as a Storyteller because He told parables, which are called brief stories. It is so important that we get an understanding of God's Word. His Word is not complicated. We, as a people, make it complicated. I really would like for you to get an understanding and the significance of what Jesus is saying in this story. The Scriptures are coming from **Luke 17:1-6**. The King James Version and The Contemporary English Version:

King James Version

"Then said He unto the disciples, it is impossible but that offences will come: but woe [unto him], through whom they come!" "It were better for him that a millstone were hanged about his neck, and he cast into the sea, than that he should offend one of these little ones." "Take heed to yourselves: If thy brother trespass against thee, rebuke him; and if he repent, forgive him."

"And if he trespass against thee seven times in a day, and seven times in a day turn again to thee, saying, I repent; thou shalt forgive him." "And the Apostles said unto the Lord, Increase our faith." And the Lord said, If ye had faith as a grain of mustard seed, ye might say unto this **sycamine tree,** be thou plucked up by the root, and be thou planted in the sea; and it should obey you."

Contemporary English Version

Jesus said to his disciples: There will always be something that causes people to sin. But anyone who causes them to sin is in trouble. A person who causes even one of my little followers to sin would be better off thrown into the ocean with a heavy stone tied around the neck. So be careful what you do. Correct any followers of mine who sin, and forgive the ones who say they are sorry. Even if one of them mistreats you seven times in one day and says, "I am sorry, you should still forgive that person." The apostles said to the Lord, "make our faith stronger!" Jesus replied: If you had faith no bigger than a tiny mustard seed, you could tell this **Mulberry tree** to pull itself up, roots and all and to plant itself in the ocean. And it would!

In this particular setting Jesus compared the "Sycamine Tree to Un-forgiveness." Alexander Pope stated, "To err is human, and to forgive is divine." He stated, "A truth that still resonates in our hearts."

Forgiving others seems to be one of the hardest things some of us ever have to do. We, as a people, deny even to ourselves, the severity of our wounds. We are aware of the hurts we've experienced, and we believe the person or people that hurt us should suffer the consequences of what they have done. What's so strange about it, we feel, if we forgive them, that we are letting them off the hook. Yet, we don't want to encourage the repeated hurts.

There is an element of trust. Your trust is gradually worn off by each hurtful incident as carrying the memory of hurts that date back to when you were a child such as:

- your parents may have rejected you or abused you;
- your mother may have preferred your sister over you because she was pretty and you were not;
- your father may have made it a habit of hitting you first, and asking questions later;
- your marriage may have required you to forgive on a daily basis, even though the feeling of love was not there anymore;
- maybe you were molested and you don't understand why this happened to you;
- maybe you were abandoned and you wondered what you did to deserve it;
- maybe you were called out of your name for no apparent reason;
- maybe you were mocked because you stuttered;
- maybe you were resentful because you were told you will never be as smart as your brother or sister;
- maybe you were battered and you felt that there was no way out;
- maybe you were hurt in the church and you just can't get passed the church hurt.

Life offers us plenty of opportunities to feel unforgiving. The trouble is, un-forgiveness does more damage to us than to the one that hurt us. When we don't forgive, our hearts become hard and we don't trust anyone, anymore.

We turn sour, bitterness begins to fester, revenge takes place, and then we want the person who wronged us to suffer. And when that happens, the first thing that we say about the person is:

- "what goes around comes around."
- we say, "every dog got his day and bad dog has two."
- we may say, "that's what they get for mistreating me."
- if that's not good enough, we will try to put it off on God by saying, yeah, God is "whooping them" because of what they did to me.

God is not pleased with this type of attitude or those negative feelings. Those feelings war against the love and compassion that should characterize us as Christians, which hinders our Spiritual Growth.

Jesus says, "If ye had faith as a grain of mustard seed, ye might say to a sycamine tree be thou plucked up by the root, and be thou planted in the sea; and it should obey you."

Jesus was teaching His disciples about bitterness and unforgiveness and how to remove evil forces from their lives. He used this illustration of the "sycamine tree," so well known in the Middle East.

In researching this tree, I found out that it was known to have one of the deepest root structures of all the trees in the Middle East. Because its roots went down so deep into the earth, it was difficult to kill. It is stated, "that the hot weather and blistering temperatures had little effect on this tree because it was tapped into the water source down deep under the earth." It is said, "cutting it to its base would not guarantee its death, because its roots, hidden deep under ground, would draw from underground sources of water, enabling its keys to resurfacing again and again."

In other words: This tree was very difficult to eradicate, meaning that the root system of a sycamine tree is impossible to uproot even by an experienced bulldozer operator. This is why Jesus used this particular tree as an example of bitterness and unforgiveness.

The sycamine tree, bitterness and un-forgiveness must be dealt with clear to the roots. If not, they will keep springing up again and again and again.

The roots of bitterness and un-forgiveness go down deep into the human soul, fed by any hurt that lies hidden in the soil of the heart. That hidden source of hurt will cause evil forces to resurface in our lives, over and over and over again. It will take a serious decision for us to rip those roots of bitterness and hurts out of our heart once and for all, so they can't ever grow back in the future.

In Conclusion:

The sycamine tree and the mulberry tree were very similar in appearance; the two trees even produced a fruit that looked identical. However, the fruit of the sycamine tree was extremely bitter, (which was a black fig), I am told. It is said, "Its fruit looked just as delicious as the mulberry, (which was red and sweet).

I am told that the mulberry was very expensive. Yet, because of the cost of this fruit, the wealthier people primarily ate it. But the sycamine fig was cheap, and therefore affordable to the poorer people. Because the poor could not afford the mulberry fruit, they munched on the sycamine fig as a substitute.

What are we munching on and what are we using as a substitute? We do not want those evil forces to get out of control and start taking over. We want to get rid of all those evil forces of defeat, depression, sickness, jealousy, hatred, gossip, strife, backbiting, discord, bad attitudes, poverty, and many others.

We want to focus on love, peace, joy, humility, meekness, harmony and happiness. We are not going to allow the devil to kill our joy, steal our peace or destroy our spiritual growth, because, "no weapon formed against us shall prosper." God commands us to love our neighbors and even our enemies, because love is greater than faith and hope.. We must remember, "the battle is not ours, it's the Lord." "Weeping may endure for a night but joy cometh in the morning." We have the victory over Satan. "We are winners and not losers."

If you did not guess what disease we were talking about in our "Introduction" or the "Message" here it is: ***"It is a Bitter Disease called Un-forgiveness."***

CHAPTER 5
Beautiful Painted Pictures

L ET ME SHARE SOMETHING WITH you as to what Satan tries to do. You notice I said, "Tries to do." Have you ever thought about how he work after you have surrendered your all and all to God and especially, when you are only trying to think on pure and holy thoughts? Here he comes again to try and mess up your life. This is what he does. He will send some of those so-called friends you did drugs with, or those that you use to drink with, or supposedly hung out with, to do numerous wrong things.

Remember, I told you we are all "winners and not losers." Yet, Satan will try to make you feel as though you were during better by hanging out with your buddies, persuading you to think that nothing has changed in your life. Oh, how naïve we become when we do not trust God to see us through.

Listen, this is what Satan would do to me when I felt like things were falling apart in my life. He would send those so-called-drinking buddies over to console me and there it was, the trend would start all over again. Can you imagine the blind leading the blind? We were all heading for a deep ditch. It was just a matter of time before we all would fall in it, only some of us would not survive.

Here is another trap that he would set in front of me. He would paint this beautiful picture for me, year after year leading me to think it was God. As I would dive into it, I realized later that it was not God at all. This would make me so angry because it was difficult for me to bail myself out of different situations. It was hard for me to understand why I was so vulnerable. Of course, Satan knew this, and would always take advantage of me.

After Satan would take advantage of me, I would go to God and say, "what good am I to you or anyone?" I would also say, "I might as well go back out there with my so-called friends because you don't care about me anyway." With this mind-set, bitterness came back into my life once again. I didn't know how to war Satan off, nor did I have anyone to encourage me in a positive way. I felt all along that's because I didn't have my family around, I had no one to confide in. So, I chose the easier route to take and that was the advice from my so-called friends.

Naturally, these were my drinking partners and the only reason they would come to my rescue is because I was the so-called friend that actually furnished the drinks and the food every weekend. I barely missed a weekend out of seven years. Yet, I would suffer on Mondays trying to borrow enough money to get my daughter and I through to Friday, which was my next payday.

For some strange reason, I kept doing the same thing week after week, month after month, and year after year. Trust me, when I say this. I honestly thought this was what friends were supposed to do. Satan had pressured me into thinking these thoughts. What a mockery I became . . . Oh, what beautiful pictures Satan paints for us and sometimes we fall right into his trap.

It is so easy to get caught up in wrong doing, because Satan knows any little spark that will light the candle will make you angry or bitter. Bitterness is known as a spiritual poison by which many are defiled. It is a source of countless spiritual and physical problems in our lives today. It can be tricky to recognize because it's not a symptom or visible on the surface, like anger.

Many claim that they are not an angry or a hateful person yet that is not what bitterness is all about. Bitterness is a root problem that doesn't always manifest on the outside, but dwells inside. This goes to show us that a root is never on top; it is always deep in the surface of the soil.

Please listen when I tell you this. In other words roots do not directly show or make themselves known, but are sources of fuel for elements that are on the surface. You don't usually see a plant showing off its root system. If a plant did not have a root system, however, it would not survive. A root's job is not to manifest on the surface, but under the surface, and fuel things that are on the surface.

Think about the fuel. Have you ever had a person around you that knew you were angry, had bitterness or resented another person. They actually knew how you felt about the person and that you kept your distance from that person. Yet, the third person found a way to stir up those old feelings and keep the fuel brewing in you, until you were puffed up enough to go and tell the person.

Now the person that pushed you into attacking this person, is either standing afar off, looking on from the background, or is nowhere to be found and will deny that they had any part in the rivalry. It is so sad. They just wanted the satisfaction of seeing the person get hurt. How devious can these types of people be? I wonder, do they realize that judgment day is coming?

Here's another scenario: What about siblings getting angry at each other and refusing to speak for years. Yet, one tries to reconcile the difference and the other one doesn't want to reconcile. They often say, "Blood is thicker than water." Is that really true? How is it that we as a family will allow the enemy to come in and destroy what God has put together? Some of us would rather die than get it right. Half of the time it's something that we are trying to cover up to justify what we have done and don't want to be exposed.

Now, this is the part that gets me. We hold the grudge year after year and when we don't want to reconcile, we try to persuade the other siblings to come against the sibling that's trying to reconcile. You must learn to consider the source and keep living all that you know for the Lord. It's not that you don't love your siblings; it's just you will have to pray for them and leave it in the hands of the Lord.

If we cannot forgive, then we definitely will not see Jesus' face. The thing that really shakes me up is that we will stand before God's people and preach the Gospel like everything is going great in our lives. "The Devil is a liar." There should be nothing or no one on this earth to prevent you from forgiving someone. How cruel can a person be? That is truly Satan working in and through that person. Again, we must continue to love and pray for them because we have done all that we can do.

The Bible says, "We are to love our enemies." The Word of God does not make a distinction as to who is the enemy. And the Bible was not written for the sinners; it was written for the Saints. I don't know about you, but I was afraid to even pick up the Bible when I was set in doing all the wrong things that I was doing.

When I chose to change my life, the blinders were taken off my eyes. I could not see the righteous when I was in darkness. When I began to experience Jesus, I never knew there were so many people living for Him. I even questioned God. I asked Him, "God where did all these people come from?" It really blew my mind . . . I am telling you, this is how Satan works.

If there is a small open space for him to crawl in, watch out, because it will become larger and larger, if you don't nip it in the bud before it begins to fester. It is like water poured on the grass. If you continue to let it grow without watering it in the summer, the weeds will out-grow the grass, kill its beauty, and take over the lawn.

Yet, once you get your grass mowed and start watering it again, it will bring back the beauty and all your surroundings are beautified, as well. We must not allow blinders to hold us down. Start asking God to remove the scales from your eyes so you may see His beautiful creation and feel His heavenly presence. It is your choice. Some people will die not seeing the beauty of God's creation right here on this earth. The enemy knows that you will experience a transformation as never before. Like a caterpillar to a cocoon, from a cocoon to a butterfly . . .

It is the best feeling in the world and that's why Satan does not want anyone to experience it. He would rather we come against each other over something petty which will escalate into something devastating, and may destroy a whole family. He preys on our weakness. I've often heard people use this terminology by saying, "We give the devil too much credit." I've never understood that phrase.

How can we give the devil too much credit? Either he has us or he doesn't. I've said it before and I will say it again, "This is a two way journey and we must make a choice as to whom, we will serve." Will it be God or Satan?" Again I say, "Satan knows that you will experience a transformation as never before."

CHAPTER 6
From A Cocoon to A Butterfly

I WOULD LIKE TO SHARE A story with you that often touches my heart and brings tears to my eyes, as it has been told down through the years in messages that God has allowed me to present to his people. It's based on how my baby sister was treated when she was living for the Lord as a teenager. This story is told how it actually happened.

As we look back over our life, we can attest to some things we have done to people, which may have brought shame into our lives. We cannot undo what we have done but we can try to make amends. There is always a solution to our shame and that's first, repenting to God and asking Him to forgive us, as well as asking the person that we have wronged to forgive us. If the person is not willing to forgive, the Bible says, "You are to shake the dust from your feet." In other words, if they don't accept it, you are to move on," just to paraphrase that statement.

I remember this as if it were yesterday. I was extremely cruel to my baby sister, Niecy. No doubt, she probably thinks about it every now and then, as well. This happened about 35 years ago. It's something that often plays over in my mind. It is because I couldn't understand how I could have been so rude to her. This spirit of cruelty and rudeness is hovering over the land, as well as over our children.

The reason why it's so easy for me to detect these spirits is because it's the same thing that I use to do. There are not enough discerners in operation for me. Everybody is saying, that they have a, "Word from the Lord," yet they have no discernment. I just don't understand some of the things that they say and do. I am truly puzzled by the saint's actions and how Satan uses them. And you know what's troubling me so much? We allow him to do it.

My little sister, Niecy was just a baby trying to do the right thing. She was only 16 years old and I was around 25 years old. As you can see, I should have been mature enough to know better. There was no excuse for my behavior. I could be cynical like Flip Wilson use to say, "The devil made me do it." That definitely would not be an under-statement for me because it is actually, truth.

My sister was living all she knew how for the Lord. I would often get behind closed doors and mock her and one of my older sisters, Ethel. It is so sad how I allowed the enemy to use me to try to keep them from living a godly life. Trust me when I say this. I've paid for what I did to them.

Yet, I wanted what they had, but I didn't want to give up my old ways. I would watch my baby sister when she didn't even know I was watching her. I wanted her to slip-up and do something wrong so I could ridicule her for trying to make people think that she was so saintly and holy.

I couldn't understand it but I knew that there was a huge change that had taken place in her life. I thought I was losing her as my friend, because we were very close and are still extremely close. She knows that there is nothing that I will not do for her or any of my other siblings. I truly love all my brothers and sisters. It's an honor to have so many of them.

Now that I think about it, I was jealous of the relationship that she had with God. Oh, I repent to God for my sins because I didn't know any better at the time and I will repent to my sister for realizing the problem was jealousy, which is as cruel as the grave. Yet, she had something that I wanted, and I didn't know how to get it.

What was extremely difficult for me to understand about my sister at the time of the change, she became so beautiful inside and out, living for God, and she's still beautiful to this day. But it seemed as though this great change took place overnight in her life. All of sudden, her skin tone totally changed; she was a different person; she carried such a beautiful glow; her hair grew longer and it looked healthier. Her nails grew, she stopped wearing pants, her attitude changed and she was as humble as a sheep. She even read her Bible quite often and she went to church all the time. That's what Salvation does to you!

To be frank, in my mind, I thought she was too young, to be doing these thing. I felt like she should be out there with all her peers having, a so-called good time. How cruel of me to have let the enemy speak to me by trying to manipulate a sweet, innocent child from serving God. Who in their right mind would do such a thing? That goes to show you that I could not have been in my right mind. This is why my heart goes out toward our young people. Because of my ignorance in the past, 35 years ago, I refuse to allow anyone to mistreat a child that wants to live for God.

I have often thought about the transformation that took place in Niecy's life down through the years. Watching her was like looking at a butterfly that transformed out of a Cocoon right before my eyes, and it was the Holy Spirit that beautified her.

It took me years to get what she had and I can truly tell you that I received it many years ago, and will not trade it for all the money in the world. Not one dime is worth what God has allowed me to experience in this Christian walk with Him.

Oh, my sister has forgiven me down through the years. She never had any animosity toward me because she loves me and she knew that it was an act of Satan. My sister's heart is kind, if she could take it out and give it to someone, she would because that is who she is. Niecy has nothing but love for God's people. This is why we get along so well, because our hearts are much alike, and we love God. **I love my sister and I thought this would fit her in a unique way. It's called "The Butterfly."**

CHAPTER 7
The Butterfly
Author Unknown

From the caterpillar to a cocoon, from a cocoon to a butterfly;

When the time of maturing in the cocoon has been reached,
the coverings part to allow the escape of the perfect insect.

The butterfly is protected from enemies by having colors,
which enables it to elude observation.

We, too, like the butterfly were wrapped in the cocoon of sin,
but one day we saw the beauty of the Lord. We accepted Him
as our Savior—and came forth as new creatures in Christ Jesus.
Old things are passed away and we now see all things new.

As the butterfly made its transformation from the caterpillar to
the butterfly—we too, make our transition from a sinner to a
saint through Christ Jesus.

As the butterfly is protected from its enemies by its beautiful
colors—we are protected from our enemies
by the power of Jesus.

As the butterfly soars above the dust—we, too, must soar above
the dust and dirt of this world such as pettiness, backbiting,
backstabbing, greed, slothfulness, jealousy, envy, strife, anger,
bitterness, pride, and deceitfulness.

We are new creatures in Christ Jesus!!! We are different!!!
(II Corinthians 5:17).

★　★　★　★　★　★　★　★　★　★　★　★　★

In Conclusion to this story: The analogy that I would like
to use is: Even though, we feel that things are getting better for
us because of the big change that has taken place in our lives. It
feels like the weight has been lifted off our shoulders from all the
wrong things that we have done. We feel like we have gotten it
right with everybody and it seems that the grass looks greener on
the other side. But we fail to remember that there are still some
"Secrets that should be exposed."

Satan will let you enjoy your high on Jesus for a season but
trust me, he will come back. A season could be a moment or
many years. The Bible says, "One day is like a thousand years and
a thousand years is like one day in God's eyesight." So now, how
do we deal with our secrets? I've come to a conclusion. Just expose
them and this will put the devil to shame. We cannot allow him
to win . . . As, Pastor Crefelo Dollar says, "We Win."

CHAPTER 8
Secrets Exposed
(Evaluate your Secrets before exposing them)

WE OFTEN FEEL AS THOUGH we can confide in a friend or family member with our so-called secret. Yet, when that person gets angry with you, they feel that it is important that the whole world should know what you have shared with them. Let me tell you, that person was never a friend from the beginning. That was Satan using that person to get information about you. In the end that person will be judged for what he or she did to you.

Some of us will actually hold on to that promise and carry it to our graves. Back in the days of old, some would rather have had their tongue cut out, as opposed to telling a secret that someone had shared with them. Some secrets are to be exposed and some are not! You just need to know which ones. Question: What if exposing a secret depended upon saving the life of the person that confided in you? What would you do? Ponder on that for a moment.

Let me assure you that there are no secrets that God doesn't know. Some, He may reveal, and some, He may not. He said, "He will not allow us to be put to shame." Some of us are begging God not to expose some of the things that we have done way back when. Do you believe every one of us has a secret that we will carry to our grave? Do you also believe that some things should be exposed to help remove bitterness and un-forgiveness out of our lives so that we may be delivered and set free?

There are so many innocent people that have even gone to prison for others for not exposing the truth; many have lied for others for not exposing the truth, and many have died for others for not exposing the truth. Exposing secrets may help a relationship or it may destroy it. It may build a family or destroy it. People may come against you, or people may love you when you start exposing some things. It is important to seek the Lord in whatever you do.

The important thing is forgiving the person/people or them forgiving you. It works both ways, yet, if you have asked that person to forgive you and they refuse to do so, that is between them and God. You have done what you were supposed to do. Now it is time for you to move on with your life. Consider this: it is not you with the problem it is that person's self-pride that's preventing them from forgiving. Can you imagine how God feels about this person? It just breaks my heart that someone could be that cruel.

God forbid if you decide to open up and expose your past life to others. Trust me when I tell you this. There are always those that will be waiting to ridicule you with sharp and bitter words by trying to discourage you and make you think that you did the wrong thing. Please be aware of those people because they are the ones that have hundreds of skeletons in their closets.

If they are not coming to encourage you in a positive way, do not receive any negative from them. You do not have to receive everything someone is telling you. Remember, "Sheep come in wolves" clothing. Know that they are working under the directions and the instructions of Satan. This is what Satan is telling them to do because he knows that you are very vulnerable by coming out of the closet. Don't let anyone deceive you from doing what is good and pleasing unto God.

In my research, I found out that it is imperative that we expose some things because holding on to some secrets causes grudge, anger, bitterness, sickness and the end result may sometimes lead a person to insanity or suicide if Satan has his way. But the "devil is a liar," and you will be free. If God did it for me, He will do it for you. He loves us all the same unconditionally . . . He's a God of "no respecter of persons."

Sharing different things in my first book ("I Don't Take It Lightly") has given me a sense of encouragement and serenity to share another secret with you. Of course I've repented to the person that I did the wrong to before bringing it to you. My slate is clean because I've repented to God numerous of times but that didn't make it right, until I exposed the secret to the person that I was withholding it from . . . .

Part I
A Secret Exposed What If?

At the age of 17, I met a young man by the name of S.L. We started dating during the last semester of my junior year in high school. My parents were pleased with him because he was very respectful and they trusted me to go different places with him. In my day, the young man would have to prove himself to the family, before a girl had permission to go out with him.

I could never meet a boy outside of our home. Due to our family's tradition, the boy had to come and ask the father for permission to date his daughter. The boy would need to visit the home a few times before he could actually take the daughter on a date. This gave the dad a chance to see if the young man was responsible and suitable enough to actually date his daughter. We don't see that today. It's called honor and respect to the family, "An action of trust."

This young man was a guitar player and he played with different groups. Being young, this was exciting for me to be dating a guy that played in a band! The relationship grew stronger, yet we had to break it off during my senior year in high school for other reasons. It was a hard decision for us to make, but it had to be done because of a commitment that was given, not thinking of the consequences that we would endure later.

We didn't realize the extent of the deep hurt that it would bring, not just in his life, but in my life, as well. I had to live with what I had done to him, which caused torture in my life for 43 long years. I felt as though I could carry this secret to my grave. After all, the relationship was over and we didn't think that we would ever see each other again . . . The things we do when we are young can follow us to our grave if we are not careful. It's our choice, yet we always try to blame others, to justify ourselves for the bad decisions that we make.

This will be the first time that my family is hearing about this, because I've never exposed it to them. Just recently this year 2011, I shared it with a couple of my sisters. I tried sharing it with my daughter down through the years but she never took me seriously. So I concealed it in my heart by wondering what if . . . .

Just before the break up, my little body was beginning to change. I was a hundred and five pounds and I jumped to a hundred and ten pounds. I thought I was just picking up weight from eating too much. But that wasn't the case.

The story begins: On a particular Friday night, we were told that there was a dance coming to town where all the teenagers hung out. I got permission from my parents to attend. Earlier that day I had started bleeding, which was the natural procedure but somewhat strange. The chills and shakes were unbelievable even though it was summertime. After all, it was almost 3 months. I thought I was just late, which was the norm for me. I decided to overlook it, because I wasn't going to let anything stop me from going to that dance.

I will never forget this night as long as I live. As I started to dance, it looked as if the building was spending around. One of the worst pains of my life hit my stomach and I could feel the blood running down my leg, along with something strange passing, as I passed out. I was taken to the same doctor when I was pregnant with my daughter, Shauntae. I told him, which is stated in my book, "I Don't Take It Lightly" that, "I felt like I had a rolling tumor in my stomach." He said to me, "yes and it's going to come forth in 9 months." This doctor announced to me that, "I had lost my baby on this Friday night," which would have been my first child.

He told me that he would need to report this to my father. I begged him not to tell my dad, because I knew I would be in trouble if he did. He said to me, "someone has to pay this bill." I asked him how much it was and I promised that I would pay, if I had to sell bottles to do it? With compassion in his heart and pity in his eyes, he said, "$5.00." He saw the fear in me and he knew I was desperate.

He took my word and allowed me to go home. When I got well, I made several trips to his office by paying him one dollar at a time. When I finally paid it off. He said, "your debt is paid in full and your secret is safe with me." That doctor took that secret to his grave and gave me an opportunity to expose it 43 years later. I will never forget those words. He taught me the true value of holding on to precious memories.

As God allowed me to share and repent to my baby's father 43 years later, we wept, yet, it was a chapter that was finally closed in my life, and it felt as though the weight had been lifted off my shoulders. I don't have to carry this burden anymore. I felt free and released. We both are married with children and I wouldn't trade my life for what God has done for me down through the years.

I don't think anyone could ever understand the magnitude of carrying something in your heart and mind for so many years and not being able to share it. Yet, carrying it alone just makes it worst. My life has actually changed since these two burdens (*the other one being raped*) were exposed. Remember, it is important to know what secrets to expose. Some may help and some may hurt. The choice is yours . . . .

I've often wondered about my baby, was it a girl or a boy? I wondered what would she or he have looked like through out the years. I would picture even twins in my mind, looking at the baby clothing quite often when I would go into different department stores. 43 years later I've often wondered what if . . . . I had not attended that dance, would my baby have survived? What if . . . I had stayed in that relationship, would my baby have survived? What if . . . I had told someone how I felt that day, would my baby have survived? I blamed myself year after year wishing that I could turn back the hands of time. I felt that I had aborted my child without knowing it. Only God knows.

The healing process has begun to take place, but the thoughts will never die. Yet, God blessed me with my Shauntae two years later after the incident. We serve an Awesome God that, "will never leave us nor forsake us." He always fulfills the hurt in our heart. I love God with all my heart, soul, mind and strength.

Part II
Secrets Exposed (A choice to make)

When God allowed me to expose some things in my first book, there are so many people that have begun to share their stories with me. Secrets are truly being exposed. The Chapter that I get so many calls, texts or emails on is "She Cried Rape," which is Chapter 3. When I hear the stories that come from different ones, it breaks my heart, because some of their stories are beyond recognition and the scars will be there for the rest of their lives. Yet, they have a choice. They can allow what happened to them to fester or they could forgive and go on with their lives. It is strictly their choice.

As looking up the definition of Rape, Molestation and Abuse: They all coincide.

- Rape—means to seize; take or carry off by force.
- Molestation—means to assault sexually.
- Abuse—means to treat in a harmful or offensive way; bad or improper treatment; misuse.

I would like to briefly share with you a few of their stories. Here is a line that I've always wanted to use as a little girl. "The names have been changed to protect the innocent."

1. This story is told by a young lady by name of Samonia.

It really brings tears to my eyes. She told me that her grandmother is over 80 years old and she was molested at the tender age of 7 in the cotton fields by a cousin. The family kept silent by shipping her off to live with an older sibling. While living in the home with her sister, she was molested by her brother-in-law. She was shipped back to her parents and was molested by her brother as a teenager. The same brother molested her daughters when they were young. Her sister's son molested their cousins. If that wasn't enough, the nephew, which is her sister's son, came into her home, and molested her daughters. Samonia said the family didn't talk about it because they were told to keep silent.

It didn't stop there. It went on to her grandsons being molested in the church and school. This teacher in the school system was diagnosed with HIV and gave it to one of the boys. One of the daughters went on to get married to find out later that her daughters were exposed at a very crucial age, one as young as 2, by a cousin that was 15 years old. Of course there is a lot of bitterness and hostility in this family because of the trend and no one ever talking about it. Yet, one day the silence was broken after 35 years and the cousin was exposed. The family found out that he had molested several girls in the church, only to serve a few months for sexually abusing one girl. He was never classified as a sex-offender. Doesn't this story just break your heart? Please keep an eye on your children and be careful who you allow to baby sit them.

2. This is by one of my close friend by the name of Bonita Ellen.

She said, "this was her off day from work and she was home alone." Freshly married, she moved from the south to a nice and friendly town where everybody knew each other, and always kept their doors unlocked, as well as slept with them open in the summer time. Naturally, she thought this is what they did in the Big City. She said, on this day, it was cold outside, and there was a knock on her door. The man at the door asked if he could use her phone because his car had stopped and he wanted to make a call to get someone to come out and fix it. She led him to the kitchen and as he attempted to use the phone he said he could not get through.

By now, she could feel that something wasn't right. She went to her bedroom and looked in the drawer at the gun but didn't pull it out. He, then, walked up behind her and placed his hands around her neck and started stabbing her in the head several time with a small knife. During the course of molesting her the phone rung. She told him that her husband worked right around the corner and he knew she was supposed to be home and if she didn't answer the phone he would come straight home. By the grace of God, that phone call saved her life or should I say, God allowed that call to save her life. The police were involved, but the man was never caught. She didn't want to talk about it anymore because it brought up to many memories. I can tell you this much. Some years later she saw this rapist at a stoplight. As she got his attention, he definitely recognized her and sped off. She only wanted to tell him that she had forgiven him and there was no bitterness or animosity in her heart anymore toward him.

3. A Six-Month-Old Baby.

Here's another sad story. I worked at a children's facility some years ago where a beautiful baby girl was brought in over the weekend. She looked like the picture of health. She was so happy and laughing with all the other babies. I asked the Assistant why was she brought in? It didn't look like anything was wrong with her. She told me, "her little organs had been damaged because her dad had been molesting her from the day she came home from the hospital for 6 months. Isn't that heartbreaking?

4. A Three-Month-Old Baby.

That same weekend, a 3 month old was brought in, as well. Her father had taken a pipe, hit her little arm with it, and broken it in several places. I just don't understand how someone could be so cruel to a sweet, innocent child.

5. A Pastor Story.

I want you to know that women are not the only ones that have encountered trauma in their lives. I had a conversation with a Pastor not knowing that he had a story and didn't mind sharing it. He said that at a very young and tender age a family member molested him. He assured me that he was delivered and hoped that he would be able to help someone that has gone through what he had gone through. He wasn't bitter because he had forgiven the person that wronged him.

6. Trauma at the Table.

While attending a Women's Convention, we were sitting at the table for lunch. I introduced myself to a young lady and all of a sudden we started talking about Chapter 3 in my book. I had no idea that she would identify that chapter with her life. She told me, that her grandfather molested her from the age of 7 until she was 21. She tried to find ways to justify for being older as opposed to reporting it. She was ridiculed in her hometown because the people felt that she should have known better than to go so many years without reporting it. The shame led her to move out of her own city and relocate.

It is so cruel how you are treated when it is not your fault. I assured her that it was not her fault and not to blame herself. As we continued to talk she stated that her sister went through the same thing. She moved away to escape the memories but the scars are still there. She said, "everyday of her life she ask God to forgive her." Her grandfather has passed away but the memories are extremely hard to shake.

7. The Terrible Memories are still there.

A young lady sent me an email after reading Chapter 3 in my book. She indicated that I took her back 35 years with a secret that she has not shared with anyone. She was 15 at the time and she had not even shared it with her family. She told me she had to go before the church to repent for something she didn't do and afterward was set down from the choir and usher board. She said they were taught to act as if they were the perfect family.

She was told that she messed up the family even if her daddy was abusive by touching her and her sisters and beating her momma on a regular basis. She stated, "that she lived in a horrible house and it was extremely difficult to get out."

She also indicated, "3 marriages later she was still trying to get out of that dreadful house." She tried getting out by drinking, doing drugs, religion, men, careers and acquiring material items. She just kept running from the pain in that house. By trying to get out of the house, she was kidnapped, almost strangled to death, gang raped and overdosed with drugs. She got angry and tried to burn down the house (set the apartment on fire) only to get caught up in the legal system. She took it a step farther by getting a gun and shooting 5 times at her ex-husband, who treated her just like her daddy. She stated, "she wanted to get out of that house so bad her only alternative was suicide." After the attempt, she was locked up in a mental institution, yet, a journey that she is now free from, because of God's wonderful grace and mercy!

She states, "she has repented to her momma and family for all the pain she has caused them over the years and she knows this is a continual healing process even if her daddy has passed away." She feels as though she is ready to deal with this secret after 35 years. Bitterness has ceased and forgiveness is ready to take place.

These are just a few stories that have taken place. Please trust me when I tell you there are millions and millions waiting to be told. They are only waiting for a listening ear. Such as the young lady that would like to talk about how she killed her attacker or the young man that has retaliated against his attacker.

People who haven't lived with the horrors of child molestation may find it very difficult to understand why someone would wait twenty or thirty years plus before reporting the crime to authorities. Victims have stayed silent for many reasons. There is often a combination of factors such as:

a. They are told not to tell
b. They don't know that they can get help
c. They are afraid they will not be believed

    d.   They assume the shame for themselves

    e.   They repress or disassociate

    f.   They "transcend" their abuse

    g.   They are embarrassed to come forward

    h.   They are prohibited from reporting by outdated statue of limitation laws

My prayer for a person that has been victimized in such a devastating way, is that they will find help to become free once and for all, because then; they become only memories, old ones at that, and it's time to let them go.

Our Television Show, "The Women of Vision" is, targeting people that have been abused: We are looking at the 5 key focuses of abuse such as:

    a.   Physical

    b.   Mental

    c.   Verbal

    d.   Molestation

    e.   Domestic

We are "Silent No More." It is time to speak out! We are willing to share your story with the world if you will allow us to. We are asking you, have you been in an abusive relationship? Are you a survivor of abuse?

Abuse comes in many forms. No matter which type of abuse you may have suffered, it is time to close that chapter of past experience. You must share in order to be delivered from it. It truly helps. Make that decision today. Don't carry this secret to your grave. Start enjoying your life. There are so many things you have missed because of this particular bondage. Start forming groups, and writing books. The choice is yours.

CHAPTER 9

There is a Consequence for our Actions (That's not nice!)

The word CONSEQUENCE MEANS—THE EFFECT, result, or outcome of something occurring earlier.

When speaking to young people it often allows me to reflect back on my life growing up in Arkansas. I've shared with them that some of my actions were done through poor choices or allowing others to influence me, especially, if they were bad decisions. I stress to them that it is extremely important to think before you act because quick decisions may cause sorrow, which may affect someone else's life as well. That's just common sense. We try to assure people that there is a consequence for our actions even if we make a right or wrong decision. The logic would be to just simply choose the right path. Not so, some of us will allow our pride or stubbornness to over-power us when it comes to what is right. We must be careful of the choices we make because sometimes-wrong decisions may end up as a life tragedy, which may even proceed to death. It's a matter of having respect for others. You may be surprised who may be watching you.

Here is an example: My daughter or my grandchildren are not responsible for my sins nor am I responsible for their sins. I may be wrong when I say this but this is my book and I believe I am at liberty to say how I feel and we can argue the issue later. Here goes.

I believe the impact of our sins lies heavily upon our children. They may not be responsible for our sins but if they see us drinking, partying, smoking cigarettes, angry, violent, jealous, fighting and using profanity all the time, nine times out of ten they will end up doing the same things that they saw us do. Some of the things that my daughter saw me do were thrown back into my face as she was growing up. When I asked her, "Why are you doing those bad things?" Her reply was, "I got it from you because you used to do it." I knew I had to make a change in my life because if I didn't, in my heart I knew I would lose her. I am not saying that this happens in every family but I want you to think about it. All I am saying is, we as parents must be extremely careful what we do around our children. Everything that we think is funny or cute is only leading our children to an open field to get slaughtered by the enemy and "that's not nice."

Parents, I ask you this question: what good morals or values do you think you can teach or instill in our children through this type of behavior? Or better yet, what can they accomplish? Remember, someway and somehow they will end up experiencing what they see or saw us do and if not, to God be the glory!

What really disturbs me the most is, when we discover all these things were wrong, we cleaned up our act, and feel or think we are living right, now we have the audacity to turn our backs on our children. God forbid. We don't even try to consider that they are acting out because of what they have seen us do. What truly makes my heart ache is that we began to blame them for their own actions. This is why it is so difficult for our children to get ahead. It is devastating for me to hear a child say, "if my momma and daddy don't care what I do, why should you?" There are some of us that really and truly care . . .

I've been observing some of our children who are so bitter and angry. They have no explanation why they are angry. Anger is a symptom of the "Root of Bitterness." It's a strong feeling of displeasure or hostility. To make someone angry is to enrage or provoke them. This is another one of Satan tools. Look how strong this thing can become if you allow the enemy to take over. The least little insult can cause a person to resent you when they are angry. It's a rage that causes insanity for a quick moment, and if tragedy should occur, it is a moment that you may regret for the rest of your life, a moment that you can never take back, a moment that you will relive over and over in your mind, or a moment that may even lead to death. Parents, we do not want our children to resent us and this is the reason why we must come together to pray for our children. If we don't pray, we will end up losing our children to the streets, which is a step away from a slow death and "that's not nice." Please review the Parent/ Children prayer.

A Prayer from the Parents to our Children

Father, we come to the Throne of Grace, as parents in need of your help today. We know that we have done some things that you are not pleased with when it comes to our children and we know that there has been or will be a consequence for our actions. We are standing in the gap for every parent that has wronged their children and we are asking every child on this universe to please forgive us for our actions. It was never our intent to hurt you or to lead you in the wrong direction. We as parents repent to God and now we are repenting to you. Please do not hold us accountable for our past. We ask you this question: Will you not allow anything to fester in your heart by coming against us? We are asking you to let bitterness cease and become free to do what

God has called you to do? We were wrong and we are sorry for our sins. We want you to know that we as parents truly love you because you are that special gift that God has given us to watch over and to teach you what is right.

Father, we are asking you to allow our children to make right choices. Father, we do not want our children to make bad choices like the two sons of Aaron, Nadab and Abihu in the Book of Leviticus Chapter 10 when they disobeyed You by lighting strange fire. As You took their lives You gave direct instructions that Aaron their father and brothers were forbidden to shed a tear over their death. Father, we need your help because we do not want our children to become a mockery to society. These are your precious children that you have created in your image. We believe that You will turn things around in their lives. We as parents are willing to bind together to break this generational curse, as well as every yoke that's hovering over our families and on our children lives. We believe by faith that it is done and it is so, in Jesus' name we pray! Amen!

CHAPTER 10
How to Overcome Hurts

Hurt causes mental pain; it is offensive or grievous.

XPERIENCING DIFFERENT TYPES OF HURTS is devastating, which causes an affect on the mind as well as the body. Wounds will heal but a hurt brings bitterness, pain, anger and stress. Some hurts last for a lifetime. I have seen so many families destroyed through sharp and bitter words. Some families never reconcile their differences. They will carry their bitterness to their grave. Even the children grow up with bitterness because they have been taught to hate that family member, yet they never knew what started the feud from the beginning.

Words are so easy to say after you have actually hurt a person, such as; "Oh well they will get over it or it will pass away." We fail to realize once something is said, it cannot be retrieved because the damage has already been done. It's like sending an email out. If you accidentally pressed the enter button before you edit your message you cannot retrieve it or should I say, "I have not found the button to retrieve it."

So now, you must deal with all the errors that were in your message or deal with someone calling to humiliate you for sending it out. I am sure you are aware that people are always looking for something bad about you. The bad, they always remember, yet, the good they have a tendency to forget, which is so backwards to me.

Now there is another solution if you don't allow pride to stand in your way. You can quickly resend the email with the corrections, ask for forgiveness and explain what happened in the process of sending it. By during this, you will have an upper hand on the person with the bad intentions, which will prevent an attack on you in advance.

This is the same way we should deal with hurting someone, unless it was our intent to hurt that person in the first place. If not, the quick and simple thing to do before anything festers would be to go to the person and ask for forgiveness. It is just that simple, and it's the right thing to do.

❖ There are so many hurts that we have encountered over the years such as:

- going through humiliation (which is a common occurrence)
- being discredited
- someone belittling you
- going through rejection
- being hurt by your mother or father
- being hurt by your child or children
- being hurt by a sibling or family member
- being hurt in a relationship (when you truly love that person)
- being hurt in a marriage (by a spouse, which is a deep hurt)
- hurt going through a divorce (some end in death)
- by someone lying to you
- by losing a loved one

- being hurt by someone taking a loved one's life
- a loved one dying
- through a business partner (associate)
- hurt on your job
- hurt in your school
- hurt in your home
- through domestic violence (wondering what you did wrong)
- through molestation (wondering will you ever get past the why and humiliation)
- sharp and bitter words
- A deep hurt
- being hurt in the church (which is the worst hurt of all)

❖ Surely, we all can attest to experiencing at least one of those hurts, if not all of them. Right now, someone is experiencing a deep hurt that has been so devastating that you have been contemplating suicide or taking the life of the person that took you through it. Trust me, nothing is worth taking your life or the person's life that hurt you. So many of us can attest to being in your shoes. Not once but many times. It was only because we felt that no one cared or we had no one to talk to about our problem. Having hope was the farthest thing from our minds at that moment. We remembered wanting to die or just crawl into a hole, never to come out. The pain and hurt was so intense, deep and strong, that there were actually voices telling us to do these things. Trust me, it definitely wasn't the voice of God. We then discovered that this was not the right attitude and we knew it would not solve the problem. So we came to a conclusion that we were better than that, and we vowed to hold our heads high no matter what the outcome would bring. I am

sure there are some folks out there that are in total
agreement with me . . .

This is called struggling with the "Root of Deception." The
reason we struggle with this pain is because there is a deceiver
(Satan) that often tries to test our faith. He is constantly whispering
in our ear on a daily basis trying to persuade us to do wrong
things. That's his job and he does it well. Not that we are giving
him credit but if we allow him to win then he will get the credit.
Do you agree?

The Bible says, *"He is a liar, and the father of it."* We must
recognize (identify) that there is a struggle within in order to
receive deliverance.

The Five Primary Forms of Deception are: Lies, Equivocation,
Concealment, Exaggeration and Understatement:

1) Lies—is making up information or giving information
   that is opposite or very different from the truth.
2) Equivocation—is making an indirect or contradicting
   a statement.
3) Concealment—is omitting information that is
   important or engaging in behavior that helps hide
   relevant information.
4) Exaggeration—is an overstatement or stretching the
   truth to a degree.
5) Understatement—is downplaying or minimizing the
   truth.

There are so many of us that conceal our pain and suffering
by trying to cover it up, bury it, hold it in, bottle it up, lock it
up, withhold it, disguise it and keep it in. It is as though we are
in denial and the truth is far from our minds because of the deep
and intense hurt we have experienced. We cannot allow defeat to
take over our lives. The mask has to come off if you want to be

free. God has given us ALL a measure of faith, which is something that we cannot see. The key is to believe that it will happen. If we trust Him it will come to past. I would like to share a message with you titled, "Your Faith is a terrible thing to Waste."

CHAPTER 11
Introduction To: (Your Faith is a terrible thing to Waste)

THERE ARE FOUR KEY FACTORS that will bring a significant standpoint to this message and they are:

1. Healing
2. Trust
3. Hope
4. Faith

Here is the break down of what each word consists of:

* Healing—was an important part of Jesus' ministry. When He sent His disciples out to tell about salvation, He gave them a special gift—the ability to heal as He did. After Jesus left this earth, the leaders of the early church received gifts of healing. In the name of Jesus, sick people were restored to health by Jesus' followers.

- Trust—is a firm reliance on the integrity, ability, or character of a person or thing. It is something committed into the care of another, it is a reliance on something in the future and it is to expect with assurance. Trust is hope. It is simply telling us that all we need to do is believe and to trust God for everything.
- Hope—is to wish for something with expectation of its fulfillment; to expect and desire. When there is a small amount of hope it is characterized as: Hope against Hope meaning little reason or justification, which brings us to ask the question, as to why is this happening to me?
- Faith—means confident belief in the truth, value, of a person, an idea, or a thing. It is a belief that does not rest on logical proof or material evidence. The Bible Dictionary states, "that faith has two meanings:"

  1) The first one is, trusting or believing.
  2) The second one is, when the Bible speaks of "the faith" it means the Gospel of Christ, the message of Christianity.

The Bible says, "People should place their trust, faith and hope in God because He loves us very much."

CHAPTER 12
The Message
"Your Faith is A Terrible Thing to Waste"

THIS STORY IS TELLING US how Jesus heals 10 Lepers. If He did it for them surely He will do it for us. Remember, "He loves us unconditionally." He will take away the bitterness, remove unforgiveness, carry our pain, take us through the suffering and heal our hurts if we have enough faith to believe it. There is a solution to every problem and the, "Problem Solver is Jesus Christ." The Scriptures are coming from **Luke 17:11-19**. The King James Version and The Contemporary English Version:

King James Version

"And it came to pass, as he went to Jerusalem, that he passed through the midst of Samaria and Galilee." "And as he entered into a certain village, there met him ten men that were lepers, which stood afar off:" "And they lifted up [their] voices, and said, Jesus, Master, have mercy on us." "And when he saw [them], he said unto them, Go shew yourselves unto the priests. And it came to pass, that, as they went, they were cleansed." "And one of them, when he saw that he was healed, turned back, and with a loud voice glorified God," "And fell down on [his] face at his feet, giving him thanks: and he was a Samaritan." "And Jesus answering said, Were there not ten cleansed? but where [are] the nine?" "There are not found that returned to give glory to God, save this stranger." "And he said unto him, Arise, go thy way: thy **faith** hath made thee whole."

Contemporary English Version

On his way to Jerusalem, Jesus went along the border between Samaria and Galilee. As He was going into a village, ten men with leprosy came toward Him. They stood at a distance and shouted, "Jesus, Master, have pity on us!" Jesus looked at them and said, "Go show yourselves to the priests." On their way they were healed. When one of them discovered that he was healed, he came back, shouting praises to God. He bowed down at the feet of Jesus and thanked Him. The man was from the country of Samaria. Jesus asked, weren't ten men healed? Where are the other nine? Why was this foreigner the only one who came back to thank God? Then Jesus told the man, "you may get up and go. Your **faith** has made you well."

Remember: "Your Faith is a Terrible thing to Waste"

In my research briefly looking at leprosy in the 21st century some of us can identify with these attacks of the enemy by characterizing leprosy versus these diseases, sicknesses, infirmities or afflictions as to name a few such as:

- Aids
- TB
- H1-N1 (Swine Flu)

- Cancer
- Sugar Diabetes
- High Blood Pressure
- Kidney Failure
- Congestive Heart Failure
- Strokes
- Blood Clots
- Hemorrhage (Massive Bleeding)
- Aneurysm
- Rheumatoid Arthritis
- Bitterness
- Stress
- Pain & Suffering
- Heartbreak & Hurts

There are two prevalent myths about leprosy, both, are totally false. The first one is that leprosy is incurable. Truth, leprosy is treatable by using a regimen of drugs. The second myth is that leprosy is extremely contagious. In actuality, most people are naturally immune to the disease, and for those that are not, transmission is still unlikely.

Between 2003 and 2004 there was a reduction of more than 20% in new cases, down to just over 400,000 worldwide. Of the remaining cases of leprosy, the majorities are found in Africa, Latin America, and Asia. In many cultures, leprosy is viewed as a divine punishment, and those afflicted are often ostracized from society as a whole. If things continue as they are, leprosy may go the way of smallpox and polio, becoming nothing more than a historical artifact.

The Letter

This letter is addressed to you. I would like to start it off by saying:

Greetings,

As I bring this story to today's terminology, I would like for you to visualize yourself in the 10 lepers setting. I want you to picture them on the side of the road, where they had been thrown out of the camp away from their husbands, wives, children, families and friends.

I want you visualize in your mind a husband not being able to embrace his wife, a wife not being able to caress her husband or a mother not being able to hold her child because of this drastic disease.

I want you to feel what they felt, such as: hopelessness, discouragement, abandonment and humiliation.

I want you to hear their cries as they were in pain every day of their lives. They didn't have pain pills to help with the pain.

I want you to imagine perhaps they woke up some days and probably saw a missing finger, a missing toe, an eye or even their nose may have rotted off. They had no hope and they thought no one cared.

I want you to visualize them carrying a stench that was so foul, that no one could stand to be around them. Or better yet, no one wanted to be around them.

I want you hear the mocking, the laughter and seeing the finger pointing as they yelled, "unclean, unclean, unclean," before they actually approached someone.

Oh, I can attest to what these poor people went through or going through in this day and time. Oh yes, leprosy still exists just not as bad as it was back then.

I am reminded by looking back on my life 30 years ago. I, too, was just like them. I could feel the parasites eating away some of the organs in my body (a tormenting spirit). I've experienced the mocking, the laughter and the humiliation of people talking about the odor that came through my pours that I had no control over. No matter how many times I bathed a day, the stench still wouldn't go away.

I've experienced the rejection of no one wanting to be near me because of the cancer battle. This is why I often hug people and tell them that I love them because I don't want anyone to ever go through what I've gone through.

Now, I want you to ponder on this phrase thinking of yourself by saying, "that could have been me." This is why I say, "**Your Faith is a terrible thing to Waste**" because we are to **"Walk by Faith and not by Sight."**

Referring back to the story in your letter that I am writing to you, please remember the setting. On His way to Jerusalem, Jesus went along the border between Samaria and Galilee. As He was going into a village ten men with leprosy came toward Him. They stood at a distance and shouted, "Jesus, Master, have pity on us!"

Jesus looked at them and said, "Go show yourselves to the priests. On their way they were healed. When one of them discovered that he was healed, he came back, shouting praises to God! I would like to picture in my mind that his shout was! "When I think of the goodness of what He has done for me, when I think of His goodness of how he has set me free, I can dance, dance, dance, dance, dance, all night!"

He bowed down at the feet of Jesus and thanked Him. The man was from the country of Samaria. Jesus asked, "Weren't ten men healed? Where are the other nine?" Why was this foreigner the only one who came back to thank God? Then Jesus told the man, "You may get up and go. Your faith has made you well." Remember, we are talking about faith. If God did it way back then, He will do it for us today.

I often tell people God does not change. The Bible says, "That He changes not." It also says that, "He is the same God, yesterday, today and forever." I thought about this. The Bible says that, "One day is like a thousand years in His sight and a thousand years is like one day." So that means, that could be any moment, but it depends on our faith. Another thought came to my mind. This is the same God:

- That parted the Red Sea and allowed the Israelites to walk through on dry ground.
- The same God that sent Manna from Heaven to fed 3 million people.
- The same God that dried up the Jordan River and allowed the Israelites to pass over on dry ground.
- The same God that told the Sun to stand still and the Moon to stay while Joshua was fighting a battle and won the victory.
- The same God that hung the Sun, Moon and the Stars on nothing.
- This is the same God that allowed a Donkey to speak.
- This is the same God that healed the Woman that had an issue of blood for 12 years. Yet, she had enough faith to believe if she touched the hem of His garment that she would be made whole.

This is the same God that we sit under today. Remember, He is a God that changes not. He's the God of yesterday, today and forever. Meaning, He is, the past, the present and the future. If He healed the ten lepers way back when, why can't we trust Him for our healing? **"Your Faith is a Terrible thing to Waste."**

When God gave me the title: **"Your Faith is a Terrible thing to Waste."** Here we go. I didn't understand at the time and I questioned Him about it? Here is the answer: He showed me, "when He heals and delivers us of certain conditions by faith, we turn around, not believing, by going back to the same state again. God is telling us, "to hold on to our faith and to trust Him for our healing." He said, "With His stripes we are healed." Why is that so hard for us to believe? God is not a liar, if He said it, He is going to do it and it's a done deal. We must place our Faith and Hope in God.

The Conclusion of your Letter
I would like to tell you a story about Faith and Hope.

As they were walking down the road one day they met at a crossroad called Key Corner. Faith told Hope, "to meet him on the other side of the Jordan River because there were some people he needed to talk with on the Riverbed."

- As Faith started on his journey a couple of miles down the riverbank he saw Misery setting on a log all by himself. He yelled, "Hey, Misery! Why are you sitting out here all alone? Misery said, "I'm waiting on my company because you know misery loves company." Faith told him, "You don't need any company." He said, "All you need is a lil'bit of faith, so come on and go with me."
- As Faith and Misery walked down the riverbank they saw Depression standing by, just watching the water. Faith yelled out, "Hey D! What you doing out here all by yourself?" He said, "I was contemplating on going into the river and letting the current take me under because there's no hope for me and no one cares." He said, "My wife filed for a divorce, I lost my job, my home, and my children, so there is nothing left for me. I am now homeless and no one wants to take me in. My friends have deserted me. When I was helping

them it was okay, but no one can help me now. Faith said, "All you need to do is trust me by having a lil'bit of faith, so come on and go with me."

- Well, Faith, Misery and Depression went on down the riverbank. Depression looked to his right and he said, "That look like Suicide sitting out there all by himself." Misery asked, "What's that he's pointing at his head?" Faith said, "It's a gun and he's getting ready to kill himself." Faith yelled! Hey Susee! What are you getting ready to do with that gun? He said, "I am getting ready to take my life. He said, I used to be a Pastor of a large congregation and I've disappointed everybody. Being the backbone for everybody, I had lots of money and a good job. I got caught up in drugs and alcohol and I can't find my way back. So the best thing for me to do is to take my life." Faith told him, "No, I can't let you do that because there is hope for you. All you need is a lil'bit of faith, so come on and go with me."

- As Faith, Misery, Depression and Suicide traveled on down the riverbank they saw a woman by a small grave just weeping. Suicide asked Faith, "What do you think is wrong with her? Look at her eyes. They are black and blue. What about that small grave? It looks like a child's grave!" Faith said, "She buried her child some months ago due to domestic violence. The little girl went to her mother and told her that the boyfriend had been molesting her. The mother didn't believe her. When the mother confronted her boyfriend about it, a violent fight broke out between the two of them. The little girl jumped in the middle to try to stop the fight and the boyfriend killed her. Now the mother blames herself for her daughter's death." Misery, Depression and Suicide asked Faith,

"Could he help her?" He said, "All she need is a lit'bit of faith. Woman, come on and go with me."

So you see, it doesn't matter what you are going through, there is hope for you. God said that:

- He will never leave us nor forsake us.
- He is the Lord of lords.
- He is the King of kings.
- He is the Lily of the Valley.
- The Bright and Morning Star.
- He is Alpha and Omega.
- He is the First and the Last.
- He is the Beginning and the End.
- He is the Great I AM.
- He is our Hope for Tomorrow.
- He said, "I AM everything you need."

Hebrew 11:1 says, "Now faith (meaning right now, this hour) is the substance of things hoped for, the evidence of things not seen."

In other words: We may not be able to see those things right now, but if we believe God, He will definitely bring them to pass, if it is His will. The key is to believe!

I pray, as you read this book, you have let go of that dreadful, "Bitter Disease Called Un-forgiveness." It is time for you to enjoy the beauty of God's creation. Receive all that God has for you, because there is a plan and a purpose for your life! You were made in His image. He loves you unconditionally and I love you too! Be blessed!!!

Special Thanks to Supporters

Seeking for the Future, Inc.

Bishop Roy & Starrie Dixon

City of Hope International @ Faith Chapel

New Beginnings COGIC

The Women of Vision Television Show

Jolee & Company

Karyes Stockdale, (my best friend) always giving me a word of encouragement.

The Southern California Fourth Ecclesiastical Jurisdiction

Stockdale's Fine Southern Cuisine Restaurant

The Hardrick's Family

The Smith Family

The Flowers Family

The Berean Christian Bookstore

KURS San Diego Gospel Radio Station

Monitor Newspapers

About the Author

JoAnne Smith Hooks holds a master's degree in theology. A native of Marianna, Arkansas born to a family of twenty siblings, she is the tenth child of sharecropper-parents, Wesley and Willie Mae Smith.

At the age of seven, she cried out to God and sought answers about her education. She was permitted to go to school on the rainy days only because she had to work alongside her parents in the cotton-fields.

When she was eleven years old, she heard the voice of the Lord, but she did not understand the call at that time. She fully surrendered her life to the Lord at a noonday prayer meeting, seventeen years later, when she heard the voice of God once again. God then sent Jesus to lay hands upon her and He told her, "I have anointed you to preach the gospel." Not once, but twice in that same hour, hands were laid upon her and she was filled with the Holy Ghost all in one day!

She rejoiced: "What a glorious experience, a day I will never forget!"

- Husband: Lee Andrew Hooks
- Daughter: Rhonda Shauntae Ramsey

Grandchildren:
- Chaquita Shaunye' Johnson
- Rodney Dwayne Page, Jr.
- Anthony Davonte Ramsey
- Lamont Terrell Ramsey

Greatgrand children:
- Kahmari Jolee'n & Kahlil Tay'Shawn Page

JoAnne Smith Hooks is a:
- Member of City of Hope International @ Faith Chapel under the leadership of Pastor Terrell & Sheree Fletcher in the city of San Diego, CA.
- The Southern California Fourth Ecclesiastical Jurisdiction Supervisor under the leadership of Bishop Roy Dixon.
- President of "Calling All Mothers" (CAM).
- Founder of "San Diego Youth Explosion."
- Producer & President of "Women of Vision Television Show" broadcast on two channels in the county of San Diego.
- CEO of Seeking for the Future, Inc.
- CEO of Jolee Books & Company.
- The Author of 2 books title, "I Don't Take it Lightly" released in 2006 & "The Root of Bitterness Workbook" released in 2009.
- Has a Master's Degree in Theology.

Editors:
Pastor Carolyn Nichols

Mrs. Louise Mothershed

Mrs. Janie Logan-Bell

Photographer:
Mr. Mike Norris
San Diego, CA

Bible References and Quotes:
King James Version
Thomas Nelson Publishing Company

Contemporary English Version
American Bible Society

The Picture Bible Dictionary
Berkeley & Alvera Mickelsen
Chariot Books

Research & Bible Quotes:
Rick Renner Ministries

John J. Eckhardt
Crusaders Ministries

Bible.org
Vickie Kraft